How We Make Our Books - *You may not have noticed, but this book is quite different from other softcover books you might own. The vast majority of paperbacks, whether mass-market or the more expensive trade paperbacks, have the pages sheared and notched at the spine so that they may be glued together. The paper itself is often of newsprint quality. Over time, the paper will brown and the spine will crack if flexed. Eventually the pages fall out.*

All of our softcover books, like our hardcover books, have sewn bindings. The pages are sewn in signatures of sixteen or thirty-two pages and these signatures are then sewn to each other. They are also glued at the back but the glue is used primarily to hold the cover on, not to hold the pages together.

We also use only acid-free paper in our books. This paper does not yellow over time. A century from now, this book will have paper of its original color and an intact binding, unless it has been exposed to fire, water, or other catastrophe.

There is one more thing you will note about this book as you read it; it opens easily and does not require constant hand pressure to keep it open. In all but the smallest sizes, our books will also lie open on a table, something that a book bound only with glue will never do unless you have broken its spine.

The cost of these extras is well below their value and while we do not expect a medal for incorporating them, we did want you to notice them.

Algrove Publishing Limited
36 Mill Street, P.O. Box 1238
Almonte, Ontario, Canada K0A 1A0

Telephone: (613) 256-0350
Fax: (613) 256-0360
Email: sales@algrove.com

Library and Archives Canada Cataloguing in Publication

Williams, J. R. (James Robert), 1888-1957.
    Classic cowboy cartoons : from his "Out our way" series / J.R. Williams.

(Classic reprint series)
ISBN 1-897030-15-0 (v.1).-ISBN 1-897030-20-7 (v. 2).--
ISBN 1-897030-29-0 (v. 3).--ISBN 1-897030-35-5 (v. 4)
    1. American wit and humor, Pictorial. 2. Cowboys--Caricatures and cartoons.
I. Title. II. Series: Classic reprint series (Almonte, Ont.)

NC1429.W573A4 2004c   741.5'973   C2004-904421-4

Printed in Canada
#1-9-05

Publisher's Note

One of the reasons J. R. Williams' cartoons were popular from the very beginning of his cartooning career is that he based his cartoons on real life experiences. He had been a cowboy, a machinist, a cavalryman, a stoker for a railroad, and a cook's helper. He struck a responsive chord in readers because he had a sure touch for detail and mannerisms.

James Robert Williams was born in Halifax, Nova Scotia, in 1888 and his family moved to Detroit when he was only a year old. He went to school only to the fifth grade before apprenticing as a machinist in the Morgan Engineering shops in Alliance, Ohio, at the wage of 6 cents per hour. By the age of 15 he had left the machine shop and was a stoker on the Pennsylvania Railroad. He then drifted for a year or two doing odd jobs, including being a muleskinner in Arkansas and a cook's helper on a road grading gang. As this wore thin, he moved on to Oklahoma where he worked as a chuck line rider on a number of small ranches.

At the age of 23 he went back to Alliance as a fireman on the Pennsylvania Railroad. Shortly, he signed up for a two-year hitch in the U.S. Cavalry where, among other things, he did free lance tattooing, boxed as a middle weight and was a member of his regiment's trick riding team. During this time he also played football with a young officer named Patton, who went on to become the famous General Patton of the Second World War.

During a trip to Chicago with the regimental riding team, he met Lita Keith and they married when he left the cavalry. He spent a short stint as a baggage handler, then as an apprentice sign painter and finally took his bride back with him to Alliance where he once again went to work in a machine shop, drawing cartoons in his spare time.

A few years after his return to Alliance he got a part-time job as an artist with Federal Developing Company, a firm that produced animated films for a number of advertisers. When that company failed, Williams returned to the machine shop. After another six years in the machine shop he was laid off and had to look for a job elsewhere, working for a while in a boiler room job where he chipped scale, replaced tubes in boilers, and shoveled coal. In his concern to develop greater security for his wife and their two small children he was on the verge of joining the local police force when he received an offer from NEA syndicate to carry his cartoons. His first "Out Our Way" cartoon was published March 20, 1922, and the success of it soon had the cartoon carried in newspapers all over North America. At the peak of his popularity the cartoons were carried in some 700 newspapers. He finally had the security he had been looking for and bought a ranch near Prescott, Arizona, in 1930 and moved there to live sometime in the early 1940s, although he still maintained a residence in Cleveland. In later years he lived in San Marino, California.

His most famous series were *Out Our Way, Cowboys, The Bull of the Woods, Why Mothers Get Grey, The Worry Wart, Born Thirty Years Too Soon,* and *Heroes Are Made Not Born.* In some of these cartoons he patterned the characters after people he had worked with. The most obvious example is the Alliance Machine Company shop foreman in his *Bull of the Woods* cartoons.

A less obvious example is the character Curly in his Cowboy cartoons. Both Curly's appearance and character were patterned after a cowboy he had worked with for some time, Frank C. Dickie who went on to later become a lawyer who, for his last 22 years of practice (1948-1970) lived in Robert Lee, Texas, where he served as Coke County Attorney for all but four years of that period. He died in San Angelo, Texas, in 1971.

Frank C. Dickie
Circa 1922

The other characters in his cartoons, Wes, Stiffy, Cooky, Cotton and Smokey might have been patterned after other specific cowboys he knew or they might have been an amalgam of various cowboys; biographical material on Williams is sparse. However, the lead character was always Curly with primary-assistant roles played by Wes, Stiffy and Cooky. Cotton and Smokey were mostly background material. Less well known and less popular was Williams' full page weekly strip, *The Willets*.

Sometime after he got into cartooning full-time, Williams met Ulmer S. Bird, a Texas poet. They exchanged letters over the years and became friends. This resulted in Bird writing a poem about Williams' work. It is reproduced on the last page of this book.

The significance of Williams' work is probably best caught in a footnote of the book, *In a Narrow Grave*, by Larry McMurtry. McMurtry, a prolific writer (*Terms of Endearment, The Last Picture Show, Lonesome Dove*, etc.) said "With Teddy Blue (*We Pointed Them North*), Haley's biography of Goodnight (*Charles Goodnight: Cowman and Plainsman*), Erwin Smith's book of range photographs (*Life on the Texas Range*) and a volume of J.R. Williams' cowboy cartoons, one can figure out just about anything one might need to know about the nineteenth century cowboy." Williams was true to his subject.

It is regrettable that we did not unearth this material on Williams earlier, but it was only after collecting and reprinting two volumes of his cartoons that we became completely besotted with his work and wanted to give all of it better context. We have included all of the factual material on him we could find.

Leonard G. Lee, Publisher
Almonte, Ontario
September 2005

Classic Cowboy Cartoons
Vol. 3
The Early Years

J.R.WILLIAMS

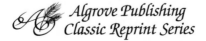
Algrove Publishing
Classic Reprint Series

Curly

Curly can be called the 'star' of the strip. He's a traditional cowboy with a big heart that extends to every living thing on the ranch, man and beast alike.

Wes

Wes is a young tenderfoot from the east seeking the romance of the old west and 'real' cowboys. He's learning the ropes but often ends up wound up in them.

Stiffy

Stiffy is an old hand who once worked with Will Rogers. He has cowboyed in Argentina, Canada and nearly every cattle state in the Union. He's set in his ways.

Cooky (or 'Sugar')

Cooky is the camp cook whose temper can be as bad as his grub. Although he and his cuisine are the brunt of many jokes, he can dish out as good as he gets. With a spatula in one hand and a pipe in the other, he doesn't take any guff.

Cotton

You will see the wonderful expressions of Cotton in almost all of the frames. He is always a willing participant when the gang plays tricks on one another.

Smokey

Smokey is another bunk-mate that you will see in almost every situation. Like Cotton, he seldom has much to say.

THE ROMANCERS

J.R.WiLLiAms

1

CURLY WOULDN'T MIND BEING CLASSED WITH
LEISURE CLASS IF HE HAD THE LEISURE.

THE CRITIC

J.P.WiLLiAMS

3

THE BULLDOGGER

J.R.WILLIAMS

"TO THE LAST MAN"

J.R.WILLIAMS

THE STAMPEDE.

J.P.WILLIAMS

THE DEMONSTRATION.

J.P.WILLIAMS

HE'S OFF AGAIN

J.R.WiLLIAMS

8

THREADIN A NEEDLE

THE TENDERFEET.

J.P.WILLIAMS

"THE SMOKE OF A FORTY FIVE"

THE SUBSTITUTE COOK.

J.P.WILLIAMS

A FALSE ALARM.

THE RUSTLER.

J.P.WILLIAMS

14

LIONS AND LAMBS.

15

THE STORM BEFORE THE CALM.

THE COLLABORATORS.

THE PESSIMISTS.

THE CRITICS

J.P.WiLLIAMS

TARPAULIN BLUES.

THE HESITATION WALTZ.

J.R.WILLIAMS

21

THE BEGINNER.

J.R.WILLIAMS

DINING OUT FOR THANKSGIVING.

J.R.WILLIAMS

23

VANISHING AMERICANS

BORN T' BE A CATTLE KILLER,
THIEF AN' GENRUL ALL ROUND PEST,
BUT I HATE T' KILL YUH, PARDNER,
'CAUSE YO'RE PART O' OUR OLD WEST.
YOU AN' ME IS SORTA BROTHERS
WITH OUR BACKS AGIN TH' WALL,
IN A ACT TH'TS NEARLY OVER
AN' TH' CURTIN 'BOUT T' FALL.

J.R.WILLIAMS

24

DRIVIN' OFF - AND ON

J.P.WILLIAMS

THE CRITICAL MOMENT

J.P.WiLLiAms

CHUCK WAGONS

THE LAMB AND THE WOLVES.

28

THE BUNKIE

J.P.WILLIAMS

THE NEW PUPIL

J.P.WiLLiAMS

THE DAILY MAIL

J.P.WiLLiAms

31

THE BOOT JACK.

J.R.WILLIAMS

THE MIRAGE

J.P.WILLIAMS

PLAYIN' FOR THE DRINKS   THE QUART

J.R.WILLIAMS

LOCAL COLOR

J.P.WILLIAMS

THE EYE OPENER

J.P.WILLIAMS

NO TIME FOR WORDS.

CHAP COURT MARTIAL

J.R.WILLIAMS

39

NIGHT HERDIN.

J.R.WILLIAMS

FOR PUBLICATION.

J.R.WILLIAMS

"THE APPLE KNOCKER"

J.R.Williams

HAVE ONE ON US.   J.R.WiLLiAMS

FIRST CHANCE ~~SALOON~~
BE POP SODAS ICE CREAM

THE COMMITTEE ON BISCUIT REFORM.

BRANDING A MAVERICK.

J.R.WiLLiAMS

45

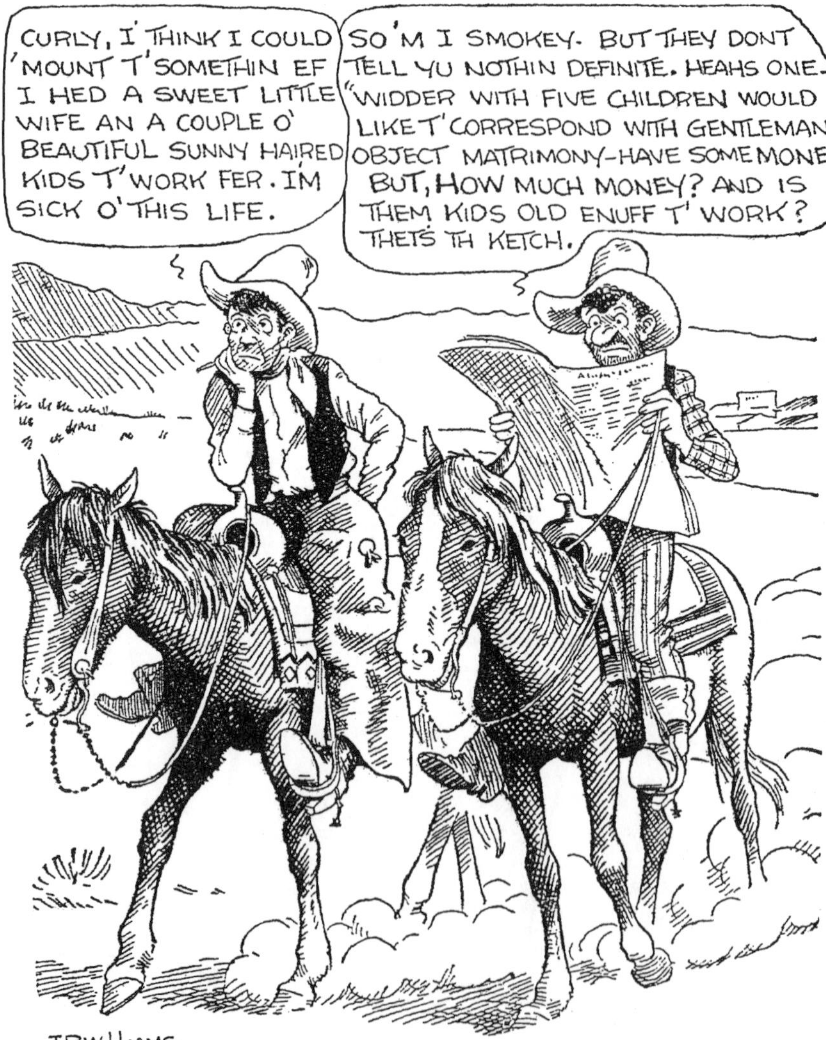

CURLY WANTS A FAMILY TO SUPPORT.

THE CONDOLENCE COMMITTEE.

J.R.WILLIAMS

47

THE BOOKWORMS TURN.

J.P.WILLIAMS

TOO QUICK ON THE DRAW.

THE STRAY.

J.R.WILLIAMS

A RUDE AWAKENING.   J.P.WiLLiAMS

THE ALIEN

J.P.WILLIAMS

52

THE SUPPORTING CAST

J.R.WILLIAMS

BORROWED PERSONALITY.

J.R.WiLLiAMS

THE SOLE SURVIVOR.

J.R.WILLIAMS

THE FOX AND THE-HOUNDS.

J.P.WILLIAMS

A RATTLING-CLOSE GAME

J.P.WILLIAMS

BECAUSE SMOKEY HAPPENS TO BE
STANDING IN THE DOORWAY IS NO REASON
WHY SCHOOL CANT LET OUT AS USUAL

J.R.WILLIAMS

58

THE NEUTRAL

J.P.WILLIAMS

59

SOUR GRAPES.

TRYIN' TO GET A RAISE IN DOUGH.

THE MAVERICK.

THE SHORT ORDER.

J.P.WILLIAMS

63

POSTING.

J.P.WILLIAMS

64

THE STRAPHANGER.

J.P.WILLIAMS

THEORY AND PRACTICE.

THE PAYDAY BLOCKADE RUNNER.

J.R.WILLIAMS

THE ENCOURAGEMENT COMMITTEE
SEES CURLY OFF FOR TEX AUSTIN'S
RODEO AT CHICAGO.

SCENTS OF TOUCH

J.P.WILLIAMS

A VANISHING ARISTOCRACY

70

THE RETURN OF THE PRODIGAL.

J.R.WILLIAMS

TURKISH ATROCITIES.

J.R.WILLIAMS

72

WHEN A FOX MEETS A FOX.

J.R.WILLIAMS

RUSHIN THE CAN

THE INTERPRETER

J.R.WILLIAMS

THE DISTURBING ELEMENT.

J.P.WILLIAMS

GROOMING THE DARK HORSE

J.P.WILLIAMS

GROOMING ANOTHER DARK HORSE

JABBIN THE GREEN EYED MONSTER

SMOKEY GETS AN EYEFUL.

J.P.WiLLiAMS

80

SMOKEY WAS TOO HASTY

J.R.WILLIAMS

81

THE SERENADERS.

J.P.WILLIAMS

THE DUKE JOINS THE OUTLAWS.

J.R.WILLIAMS

83

CIRCUMSTANTIAL EVIDENCE.

A MAN'S MAN.

J.R.WILLIAMS

CURLY 'LL MARRY FOR REVENGE, NOT LOVE

OUR BUNKIE.

J.P.WiLLiAMS

87

MISS VANCE HAS A CALLER

J.R.WiLLiAMS

NEWS FROM THE RANCH.

THE ACQUITTAL.

THE CHARACTER ANALYST.

J.R.WILLIAMS

THE EAVESDROPPER.

J.R.WILLIAMS

THE ANONYMOUS BENEFACTOR.

WHEN THE SPHINX TALKS.

J.P.WILLIAMS

OUT OF THE NIGHT.

J.P.WILLIAMS

THE PROWLER.

J.R.WILLIAMS

PUBLIC OPINION.

J.R.WiLLiAMS

THE HOUND MEETS THE FOX.

THE FAST WORKER.

THE HONEY MOONERS.

J.R.WiLLiams

NOTHIN' STIRRIN'

J.P.WiLLiAMS

THE TAKE OFF

J.P.WILLIAMS

HIGH HEELED BOOTS.

105

THE GREAT SILENT SPACES.   J.R.WILLIAMS

YOU AIN'T EVER DID REAL EATIN'
IF YOU'VE NEVER BEEN OUT WHERE
A SPUD TASTES JES LIKE HONEY
AN A SINKER'S LIGHT AS AIR.

J.R.WILLIAMS

THE HUSH OF SPRING.

108

GETTING AWAY FROM THE MAIN SUBJECT.

J.R.WILLIAMS

MISSING ON THE FIRST SHOT.

111

PANT LOONS.

WHEN THE TRUTH WILL OUT.

YOU'D SWEAR IT WAS A MIRICLE
EF YUH SAW TH' DEAD AWAKEN.
PSHAW! ANY COOK KIN DO IT
WITH A SKILLIT AN' SOME BACON.

J.R.WILLIAMS

THERE'S A KETCH TO IT.

THE ROAST MASTER.

THE DUDE.

J.P.WILLIAMS

122

FOLKS, MEET BLOSSOM.

123

THE HYPOCRITES

J.R.WILLIAMS

124

LOCAL COLOR.

J.P.Williams

OUR HERO SAVES THE DAY AND SOME LIVES.

A LOAD OF DEBT

THE WINDING TRAIL

J.R.WILLIAMS

ON THE ROAD TO THE RODEO.

THE HOME STRETCH.

HEADIN FER TH''ALTER.

J.P.WILLIAMS

THE FALL OF SOME CHAMPIONS

J.R.WILLIAMS

"LOVE'S LABOR LOST."

THE CANDY KIDDERS

They are ridin' past th' sky line, Curly, Cotton an' th' rest,
I've seen 'em turnin' westward, th' commonest an' best.
Th' humanest of humans ever seen in any land,
With ther souls an' moral natures an' ther faces full o' sand.
I've seen th' windmill fallin' near th' round up of th' past
An' I've heard th' dyin' hoof beats of a day thet could not last.
For th' ranch house in th' hollow an' th' dirt tank on th' plain,
Are crowded in a corner by th' cotton an' th' grain.
In th' glimmer on th' grainfields of a summer day I see
Phantom pictures of th' prairie an' th' things thet useter be.
So I've set 'em down on paper as they came thru memory's haze,
Just a touch o' recollection of th' silent vanished days.

Verse
by
ULMER S. BIRD

This verse by Ulmer Smith Bird appeared in the 1927 printing of 'Out Our Way Cowboy Cartoons' by J.R. Williams. In an interview, Mr. Bird had this to say about his verse, "This poem was based on one of Jim Williams cowboy cartoons and I mailed a copy to him. Soon after, I got a letter from Williams asking if he might use the poem as a frontispiece in his first book of cowboy cartoons. 'Of course', I replied, and he did."

When the book was published, J.R. presented Ulmer with an autographed copy. Their acquaintance continued over the years by frequent correspondence in letters.

'Vanished Days' by Ulmer Smith Bird (1900-1988) reprinted courtesy of Mrs. Josephine R. Bird, Texas and courtesy of the West Texas Collection, Angelo State University, San Angelo, Texas.